To Sarah
Who could always tell a good tale.

Babette Cole

Hair in Funny Places

A Book About Puberty

HYPERION BOOKS FOR CHILDREN
NEW YORK

"Ted, when will I grow up to be a 'grown-up'?"

"That depends on Mr. and Mrs. Hormone.
They are in charge of growing up."

They live inside you and are so tiny
that you can't see them.

If you could, this is what you would see.

When your mom was little
she was just like you.

And for about eleven years Mr. and Mrs. Hormone slept peacefully inside her, until her body clock woke them up! This made them very grumpy!

It was time to mix the potions that turn children into adults, and send them around her body.

Mrs. Hormone's mixtures
began to work, and
your mom sprouted
small breasts

and hair
in funny places....

Her voice deepened.

Then she found a tiny
drop of blood in her
underpants!

It meant that one day
she could grow up
to be your mommy.

Later, the bleeding started happening once a month.

Sometimes it made her feel awful.

But she was happy
to be growing tall.

The potions made her crazy about boys.

At the same time
they gave her pimples!

She worried in case
she wasn't developing
in the same way as
her friends.

But Mrs. Hormone's
mixtures do not
affect everyone
the same way
at the same time.

The stuff made her feel very up and down; some days she felt pleased with herself,

but on others she was angry with everyone.

Never mind.
She had a grown-up body,
which she liked.

Now let me tell you about your dad.
When Mr. and Mrs. Hormone
got to work on him,
he was only about eight.

To make him grow up, they worked out
a whole new chemical mixture.

They flooded his
insides with it!

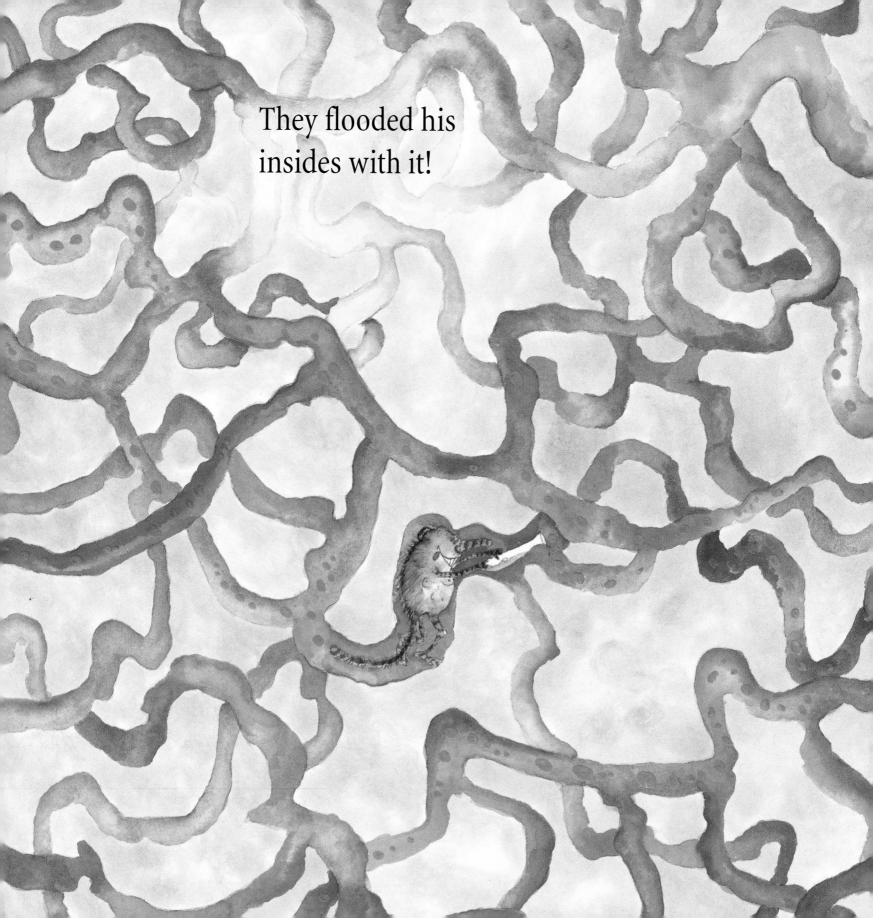

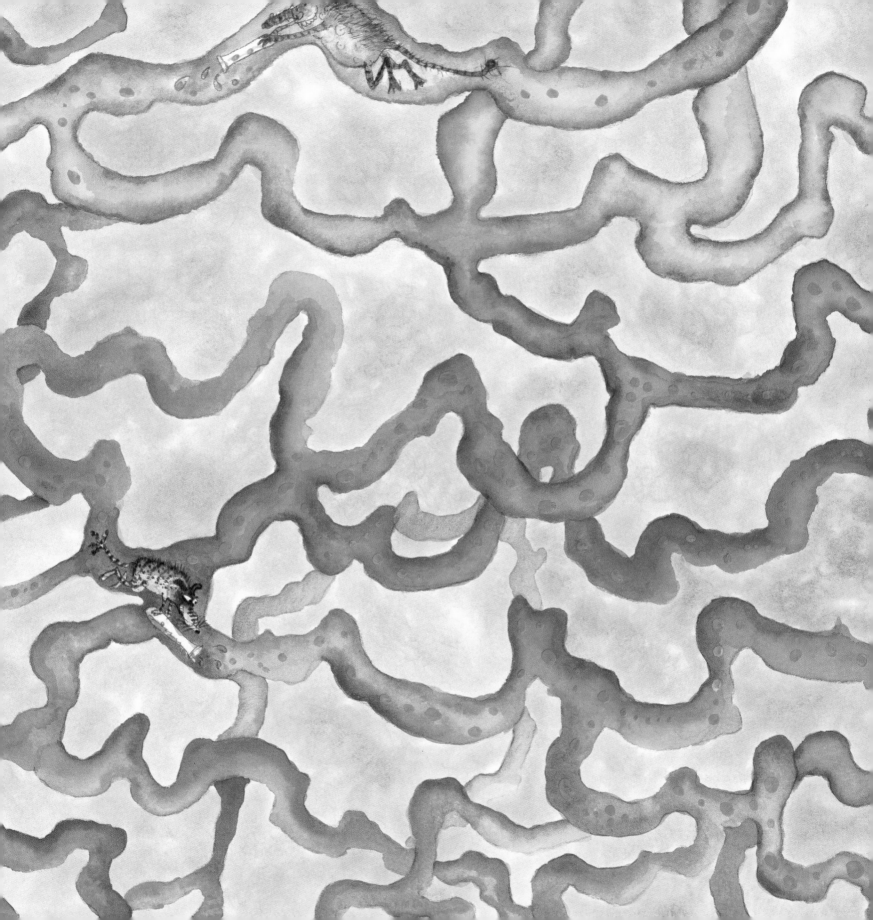

A year or two later,
his shoulders
broadened
and his penis
thickened.

He, too, grew hair
in funny places.

As for his voice,
it was deep one
minute and
squeaky the next.

He soon began
to take an
interest
in girls.

Inside his penis,
Mr. Hormone was
lurking with another
portion of the mixture.

This made it grow big and small whenever it wanted.
Then some sticky stuff actually came out.
It meant that one day he could be your dad!

He wanted to kiss girls, but Mr. and Mrs. Hormone
had made him pimply and smelly.

By the time he was eighteen, the pimples had disappeared, and he was a handsome young man.

Then Mr. and Mrs. Hormone's dog
invented the wildest potion of all.

When your mom and dad met,
the potion was sent whizzing around their bodies.

They were crazy about each other!

And they made you.

"I suppose when you grow up,
you won't want me anymore."

"Oh no, Ted, you are so wise,
I will always love you.